PROFILES OF INTEGRITY

2

Real People
Who Demonstrated
Godly Character

Marilyn Boyer &
Grace Tumas Ehrman

Master Books First Printing: January 2026

Master Books, P.O. Box 726, Green Forest, AR 72638

Master Books® is a division of
the New Leaf Publishing Group, LLC.

ISBN: 978-1-68344-430-5
ISBN: 978-1-61458-949-5 (digital)

All Scripture verses are from the King James Version of the Bible.

Please consider requesting that a copy of this volume be purchased by your local library system.

Printed in the United States of America

Please visit our website for other great titles:
www.masterbooks.com

For information regarding promotional opportunities, please contact the publicity department at pr@nlpg.com.

PROFILES OF INTEGRITY

2

Real People
Who Demonstrated
Godly Character

Marilyn Boyer &
Grace Tumas Ehrman

Credits

Thanks to the following people for their indispensable help in writing Portraits of Integrity: Grace Tumas Ehrman, for her sensitive and colorful portrayal of these heroes in writing their stories.

Mary Ann Edman who, with help from her husband Ed, produced the layout and design, along with other beautiful graphic effects. Thanks, Mary Ann, for your commitment to excellence!

And Judy Saunders, Krystyn Walker, and Grace Boyer for their proofreading work.

Chronological Table of Contents

Table of Contents by Character Quality

Introduction

Who doesn't love a good story? The Portraits of Integrity series was written to engage students (and their parents) with gripping true stories from the pages of history. Many brave and courageous men and women sacrificed to deliver freedom to future generations. May we never forget the cost they paid or take it lightly.

Reading about events in the lives of real people will teach a lot about history as a byproduct. History does not have to be boring and dry. The stories are delivered in a compelling personal way so that the readers will not be quick to forget.

As you read about the lives of these amazing people, you will be inspired to implement character qualities they demonstrated as you respond to life's many circumstances. For instance, read about the gentleness President Lincoln showed a wounded Confederate soldier and the sensitivity and genuine concern General Robert E. Lee offered to a young Union soldier who taunted him as he passed by.

I hope you will be challenged as I was by those who came before us, leaving a legacy of character as an example to follow.

Marilyn Boyer

The expedition of Messrs. Lewis and Clarke, for exploring the river Missouri, and the best communication from that to the Pacific Ocean, has had all the success which could have been expected. They have traced the Missouri nearly to its Source, descended the Columbia to the Pacific Ocean, ascertained with accuracy the geography of that interesting communication across our continent, learned the Character of the Country, of its commerce, and Inhabitants; and it is but justice to say that Messrs. Lewis and Clarke, and their brave Companions, have by this arduous service deserved well of their country.

—Thomas Jefferson, December 2, 1806
message drafted to Congress

Truthfulness

DEFINITION

Trustworthiness by accurately stating the facts

MEMORY VERSE

Hear; for I will speak of excellent things; and the opening of my lips shall be right things. For my mouth shall speak truth; and wickedness is an abomination to my lips.

Proverbs 8:6-7

Bird Woman

Sacagawea

Northwest Passage

November 1804

November 1804. The two strangers came to the lodge of the French trapper, Toussaint Charbonneau, at the Hidatsa village, on a cold winter day. Fires were burning in the rounded Mandan huts covered with turf and heavy buffalo skins. Seventeen-year-old Sacagawea, light and brown and quick as a bird, listened as the men spoke to her husband. Called the Corps of Discovery, the two men, who were bundled into warm jackets, needed a skilled interpreter to lead them through Dakota Territory and over the mountains to the east. They talked of discovering a Northwest Passage that would allow an overland trading route to the Pacific.

She spoke their strange names: Meriwether Lewis and William Clark.

She felt the child move within her as she listened. Growing up in the sweeping grasslands of Idaho as a Shoshone girl, kidnapped and held as a slave by the Minitaree Sioux at age 12, she had never seen the sea. Charbonneau began bargaining craftily with the two strangers. He would go, but only if Sacagawea went with them. The two men nodded. A woman gave an expedition a friendly tone. As a Native American, Sacagawea could also speak the Snake (Shoshone) language of the nations they passed through when they reached the headwaters of the Missouri River. She could barter for food and obtain horses.

A week later, Sacagawea and Charbonneau moved to Fort Mandan, which had been built by Lewis and Clark as a home base. Sacagawea spoke no English. Captain Clark carefully penned Bird Woman's name in his journal: "Sah-cah' gah-we-ah." At first, they thought little of her. But as they grew to respect the young Shoshone woman, Clark nicknamed her Janey.

The expedition set up a three-way translation system. Sacagawea and Charbonneau made a husband-and-wife team, translating from Shoshone to French, and ultimately to English.

Sacagawea guiding the Corps of Discovery

At 5 p.m. on the evening of February 11, 1805, Sacagawea gave birth to a baby boy. Charbonneau named him Jean Baptiste, but Clark called him "Pomp" or "Pompey." Still weak from the birth ordeal but uncomplaining, Sacagawea left Fort Mandan with the expedition, carrying Jean Baptiste in a cradleboard on her back.

The Corps of Discovery headed upriver from the Missouri as the April sun strengthened. Sacagawea, with her baby, was the only woman to accompany the 33 members of the party who headed to the Pacific Ocean. During the day, she dug up edible roots, foraged for plants, and gathered wild berries as they ripened. She made medicine from herbal tinctures. Jean Baptiste, the "little dancing boy," frolicked and laughed as he sat beside his mother in the boats or bounced between her shoulders when they switched to horseback. She helped pole up the Missouri River in expeditionary boats called *pirogues.*

On May 14th, the water, swollen with spring currents, was high and foaming. A wave crashed against the boat, tipping instruments, books, and papers into the raging yellow Missouri. While the men struggled to right the boat, Sacagawea swiftly rescued Lewis' and Clark's precious records, journals, and supplies from the water before they sank. But the medicine was lost.

William Clark

When Sacagawea fell ill near the headwaters of the Missouri, the explorers, until now indifferent to the Shoshone woman, realized how much they needed her. Without her, they could not know if the information they received was correct. They could not locate Native American guides or horses.

Meriwether Lewis

On August 12th, the expedition reached the Continental Divide at today's Lemhi Pass. It was the gateway to Shoshone country, the land Sacagawea had not seen for five years. No explorers or settlers had ever entered the Shoshone lands. Making groundbreaking history, Lewis and three other men scouted ahead for 75 miles, chopping brush and branches out of the way.

Her face showed no emotion, not even when she pointed out the place at the Fork of the Three Rivers where the Sioux captured her and killed the rest of her family. Her words related the facts truthfully and accurately without concealing anything. As the only Native American on the expedition, the only teenager, the only woman, the only mother in camp, she was an oasis: a world in herself.

On August 13th, they stumbled across a group of Shoshones. Sacagawea went ahead to meet them. As she came closer, she recognized the blankets and feathered headgear of the Lemhi-Shoshones. Sacagawea began to dance in her moccasins, waving back to Lewis and Clark. "These are my people!"

The two groups converged. Suddenly, a familiar face swam into sight. Broken images flashed through her mind.

The Minitaree swept down on the Shoshone camp like leaves swirling before a summer storm. Tipis tilted and cooking pots rolled along the ground, spilling craggy knuckles of meat. Women and children scrabbled on their knees, digging their fingers into the hot ashes as enemy horses trampled them down. Lances decorated with Sioux war feathers, flew through the air. She felt her hands jerked behind her back, tied with rawhide. Her brother Cameahwait running . . .

Now, her brother's face smiled at her between the soft black braids of a Shoshone chief. Her brother and her sister's boy were all that survived the disastrous raid of 1799–1800.

All at once, a woman rushed into Sacagawea's

arms. Lewis and Clark, standing off to one side, watched as the two women hugged and crooned. Her friend Otterwoman, captured at the same time by the Sioux, had escaped from the enemy camp and found her way home. For five years, Sacagawea did not know if she was alive or dead. In the end, Sacagawea chose not to stay with her birth-tribe. Raided by the Minitaree and Blackfeet tribes, the Shoshone found themselves forced back on poorer, barren land. She decided to continue the expedition to the sea.

While Sacagawea translated back and forth, the Shoshone braves led out strings of horses. Without horses, Lewis and Clark could not hope to locate the Northwest Passage. Because of her presence with the group, the Shoshone also sent along a couple of guides to steer them across the mountains. It would take months of trekking before they reached the west coast.

Early autumn had come. Snow fell in the upper Montana and Idaho mountains as early as July. Now, the wind whistled over the cliff faces and canyons, forcing the party to creep back to shelter. Carrying her six-month-old baby in a wooden cradleboard with a high, hooped yoke on her back, Sacagawea scrambled up the rocks beside the men. No food grew here. Slope after slope of the Rocky Mountains rose before them, never-ending, menacing. The skies turned grey and leaden with early snow flurries. Finally, the food ran out. Sacagawea and the men gnawed frozen tallow candles to survive. At last, they came down the other side of the mountains into a mild valley where Sacagawea dug and cooked camus roots for them.

November closed in on them. The expedition neared the Columbia River on the Pacific Coast. Trading with the Chinookan people there proved profitable. Lewis and Clark found the present they wanted to take back to President Thomas Jefferson as a trophy: a thick soft robe sewn from the pelts of two sea otters. The explorers wanted to trade for it, however the Native Americans refused their goods. Finally, after fruitless bartering, Sacagawea gave up her precious blue beaded belt to seal the trade.

Four days later, they reached the Pacific Ocean. When the men came back from the headland overlooking the shimmering waters, the entire expedition, including Sacagawea and Clark's Black and enslaved manservant, York, cast their votes on where to build their winter quarters: Fort Clatsop.

January 1806 brought harsh storms that washed up a whale's carcass on the beach. The men gathered tools together to scavenge the whale blubber needed for cooking fat and oil lamps. Sacagawea, who had not yet seen the ocean, demanded to see this "monstrous fish" for herself.

On the return journey, Sacagawea proved valuable as a guide. Reaching the great plain at the foot of the Rocky Mountains, Sacagawea told Clark that she recognized this place from her childhood. Clark had no idea which path to take. Remembering Shoshone hunting trails, she led the party through a road in a gap (Bozeman Pass) that wound down to the Yellowstone River without the danger and difficulty of the earlier crossing. Delighted, Clark called her his "pilot."

Crossing the Yellowstone, Sacagawea nearly drowned. The infant's clothes and mosquito netting swept away right from under her feet. She barely had time to grab her baby. Wet, cold, and shivering, Sacagawea huddled with little Jean Baptiste, who now had no blankets. Clark, fearing lest her illness come back, hurried to camp to find warm clothes for her and the small child. After more than a year on the trail, Sacagawea and Charbonneau returned to live at Fort Mandan.

Details of Sacajawea's life beyond the Lewis and Clark expedition are somewhat hazy over time. When she died remains a mystery. A fur dealer's journal entry places Sacagawea at Fort Manuel Lisa Trading Post at the mouth of the Bighorn River in 1811. Her own tribe, the Lemhi-Shoshone, maintain that she lived to be a very old woman and died among them in 1884. Historical documents suggest, however, that Sacagawea may have died prior to a Sioux Nation raid on Fort Manuel in 1812. A clerk at the fort recorded that Sacagawea died of a "putrid fever" that same year. She was twenty-five years old and left a baby girl. Records show that Charbonneau and their daughter Lizette survived the Sioux Nation's attack on Fort Manuel a few months later, but any other details of Sacagawea did not. Charbonneau handed over the guardianship of their son, John Baptiste, to William Clark while Sacagawea was alive.

Legend has depicted the "Bird Woman" Sacagawea as Lewis and Clark's guide. While it is not certain how large a role she played in leading the party to find the Northwest Passage, she did translate and report facts that helped insure the success of the mission. It is certain that she navigated more than 30 members of the expedition through the Rocky Mountains on the return journey. As a wife and mother, she worked to help her fellow explorers survive, served as a kind of ambassador to the Native American nations, and walked across half a continent with a baby on her back.

Sacagawea (right) with Lewis and Clark at the Three Forks

Sacagawea demonstrated truthfulness by translating carefully between members of the expedition and the numerous Native American groups she spoke to and guiding the expedition accurately across the Rocky Mountains.

... [Sacagawea] ...has been of great Service to me as a pilot through this Country ... recommends a gap in the mountain more South which I shall cross.

—Journal entry of William Clark, July 13, 1806

Questions

1. What incident in Sacagewea's childhood changed her life dramatically?
2. Why was Sacagewea so valuable on this expedition?
3. Why was her function of communicating with the Indigenous people groups so dependent upon her truthfulness?
4. List some ways she protected the men from potential disaster.
5. Tell of her being reunited with her brother.
6. What special hardships did Sacagewea face on this journey?
7. How was the mission of the expedition benefited by meeting up with Sacagewea's brother and friend?
8. Just how important is truthfulness in our dealings with others? Do you make a point to speak with truthfulness in your everyday life? How does your truthfulness affect those around you?
9. Think of some instances where you may not have been accurate in speaking with truth and make specific plans to correct this in your life.

Respectfulness

DEFINITION

Treating others with honor and esteem

MEMORY VERSE

Let nothing be done through
strife or vainglory; but in lowliness
of mind let each esteem
other better than themselves.

Philippians 2:3

Red Dawn

Francis Scott Key

Baltimore, Maryland

September 1814

Baltimore, Maryland: September 13, 1814. His friend was out there somewhere. Lights glimmered along the deck of the British ship *HMS Tonnant* moored off Baltimore Harbor. Vice Admiral Alexander Cochrane, Rear Admiral Sir George Cockburn, and Major General Robert Ross dined aboard. Dark, curly-haired Francis Scott Key climbed into a boat with Colonel John Stuart Skinner, the American Prisoner Exchange Agent. Without Skinner's help, he would never have located the

Francis Scott Key

right ship. They drew close up under the great black hulk looming out of the water. Inside, soft candlelight flooded the dining room as a British officer ushered them in and invited them to eat.

At first, Key had opposed this war, sparked by friendly trading with Britain's enemy, France, and the kidnapping of American sailors by the British navy. But when the war crept into the Chesapeake Bay area, Key promptly joined the volunteer militia with the "flying battery"—horse-drawn artillery. He was in Georgetown when he received the message about his friend.

Dr. Beanes was somewhere nearby. But Key's sharp lawyer's brain told him to be careful. Before fleeing, the government at Annapolis had entrusted Dr. Beanes with guarding the state records in Upper Marlboro County. The British occupying Prince George's County marched softly over the fields and roads, enthralled by the beauty of the small towns and countryside. They kept their hands off property. They did not burn homes. Except for helping themselves to large quantities of livestock, the army seemed on its best behavior after torching Washington, D.C. two years before. But to make his job more risky, Dr. Beanes had two guests at his plantation: Admiral

Cockburn and General Ross. When Dr. Beanes threw two drunken stragglers into jail, one escaped, caught up with his unit, and filed a protest. Without thinking, he had placed the whole town and the records in danger of reprisals. Shortly afterwards, one of Ross' British detachments marched on the plantation and arrested the doctor. But the state papers survived.

Francis Scott Key watching the bombardment of Fort McHenry

Key knew that he had to rescue his friend. The people of Marlboro had enlisted his help to rescue their beloved citizen. Now, Key formally asked Admiral Cochrane for Beanes' release. President Monroe had sent a vessel to use in the interests of the cartel, a formal military prisoner exchange agreement. Then General Ross spoke up. After their prowling about in the dark and aboard ship, Key and Skinner now knew the strength and position of the British navy drawn up outside the strategic Fort Henry at the mouth of Baltimore. They also knew that the British meant to attack within the next few hours. Ross would let Dr. Beanes go, but the whole party must stay under brief arrest until after the battle.

Under the autumn sky, Key clambered across the gangplank to the frigate, *Surprise,* commanded by the Vice Admiral's son, Sir Thomas Cochrane. Then, like the changing of the guard, the soldiers soon clicked their heels and spun them about in the opposite direction. They were going back to their own vessel. All at once, the bombardment began. Guns pounded from gun-ports and decks nearby, causing a tremor to go through the sloop. Staring out over the black harbor, Key could see the sky lit by red streaks and flashes. Rockets shot upward, raining down showers of sparks as they landed near the fort. All night, the explosions went on, deafening their ears. But their flag still floated in the smoky glare like an eagle over a sea of blood.

Dawn broke in crimson red. The firing had suddenly stopped a little while before. A deathly silence fell over the harbor. Key's heart beat painfully like a muffled drum. He strained his eyes, trying to see through the fog if a British or American flag flew from the fort's ramparts. Then through the smoke, he saw the tattered Stars and Stripes still flying. A thrill ran through his body. They had held out. Searching his pockets, Key found a crumpled letter. Borrowing a pen, he sat down and began scribbling madly. He had to get the words out while they were white-hot.

"Oh, say, can you see by the dawn's early light what so proudly we hailed at the twilight's last gleaming?"

Fort McHenry

Once ashore, Key handed his scrawled poem to Captain Benjamin Eades of the 27th Baltimore Regiment. Eades, who had been under fire in the Battle of North Point, dashed the copy off to press. Then with a fresh sheet in his hand, he hurried towards the old tavern standing next to the Holliday Street Theatre. Today it was full of actors shouting, drinking, reciting lines. Printed on the headlines was the tune name that Key had chosen: "Anacreon in Heaven." Captain Eades began reading the verses aloud. As he finished, the crowd began calling for music. So Ferdinand Durang mounted a chair and sang it through to the last line:

"Oh, thus be it ever when free men shall stand . . ."

Within a short time, "The Star Spangled Banner" became known throughout the United States.

Francis Scott Key demonstrated respectfulness by going to the rescue and securing the release of Dr. Beanes. By doing so, he witnessed a great event in American history and solidified it forever in the minds of Americans through his words.

O thus be it ever when freemen shall stand

Between their lov'd home and the war's desolation!

Blest with vict'ry and peace may the heav'n rescued land

Praise the power that hath made and preserv'd us a nation!

Then conquer we must, when our cause it is just,

And this be our motto - "In God is our trust,"

And the star-spangled banner in triumph shall wave

O'er the land of the free and the home of the brave.

—Francis Scott Key, the last stanza of "The Star Spangled Banner"

Questions

1. What had happened that led to Dr. Beanes' imprisonment?
2. For what reason did the British detain Dr. Beanes and Francis Scott Key after agreeing to release Dr. Beanes?
3. What did Francis Scott Key witness that night?
4. What were the British attempting to do?
5. What was Key inspired to do when he saw the flag still flying over the fort?
6. What did he use to write his song on?
7. What did he do with his song upon reaching shore? What did he title it originally?
8. Explain how Key demonstrated respectfulness to his friend Dr. Beanes.
9. How did he end up inspiring countless millions to have a respect for our country?
10. What could you do to show greater esteem for your parents? pastors?
11. In what ways could you live your life to show deeper respectfulness for Christ?
12. Specifically, what could you do to daily show a greater respectfulness for others?

Virtue

DEFINITION

Maintaining moral excellence and
setting godly standards

MEMORY VERSE

And beside this, giving all diligence,
add to your faith virtue;
and to virtue knowledge.
2 Peter 1:5

The Secret

Queen Victoria

England

1837

The London express train hurtled through the foggy, black night, the lamps shining like fuzzy orbs against the thick blanket of fog. Just then, the train shuddered to a sudden stop as the engineer caught sight of a figure, wearing a flapping black cloak, standing in the middle of the tracks. It waved its arms frantically. The wheels hissed and squealed as the engineer jammed on the brakes. He and one of his crewmen jumped down and ran towards the mysterious figure. But it had disappeared. They shouted into the night, their voices muffled by the drifting grey fog. No one answered. Puzzled, the two men fanned out across the tracks, walking further along the ties into the mist. Suddenly, they stopped short. The ground fell away beneath their feet: the bridge had washed out ahead of them. Chunks of wood and planks churned in the rushing torrent far below. Trembling, the men looked back at the train. If that strange figure had not leapt out in front of them to warn them, the crew and the passenger train carrying their dark-haired, eighteen-year-old Queen Victoria, would have plunged headlong to their deaths.

Queen Victoria and her eldest daughter

While the bridge and tracks underwent repair, the crew searched again through the countryside for the man who had flagged down the train. But no one appeared. When the news came out, no one came forward claiming to have saved the Queen's life. Then, as the crew inspected the train in preparation for its next run, they solved the mystery of that night. Taking down his lamp to clean it, the engineer found a huge dead moth squashed on the base of the lamp.

He stared at it for a moment. Then he spread its wings and stuck it against the lamp's glass. Scrambling up into his cab, he turned on his light and suddenly, he was reliving that foggy, black night again. The "flag man" stood waving in his beam. Now the engineer realized what had happened. The moth had slammed into the beam only a few moments before the train would have tumbled off the edge of the washed-out bridge. In the thick fog, it looked like a ghost waving its arms.

The young Queen listened to the investigation's report. Then she said simply: "I'm sure it was no accident. It was God's way of protecting us."

She knew that God had spared her life for a purpose. It would not be the last time. While riding in an open carriage in London several years later beside her blue-eyed German husband, Prince Albert, she came face to face with death again when a young man aimed a pistol at her. Her husband knocked the gun away with his walking stick, while his manservant, John Brown, jumped on top of the man. It happened so fast that Victoria was not even frightened.

She had come to a throne and a country troubled by the excesses of her two uncles, George IV and William, and their self-indulgent reigns. In Ireland, the Catholic peasants starved while Protestants had taken over most of the land by law since the 17th century. Others formed anarchist societies to attack the power of the British Crown over their island.

In addition, England in the 1840s had entered the age of the Industrial Revolution. Men, women, and children flowed from the rural countryside into grimy and poverty-stricken factory towns, where they ate, slept, and died in overheated, dangerous conditions within the reach of the factory whistle. The discontentment rose so high that someone had attempted to kill the queen.

When Queen Victoria came to the throne in 1837, almost no one had seen her. She would soon change that. When told that her uncle, William IV, was dead, she summed up the next 63 years of her reign in one short sentence: "I will be good." During her reign, the British Empire expanded dramatically, establishing colonies in Africa and India. Social literature, missionary societies, and the Salvation Army all emerged and flourished during what became known as the "Victorian Era." This era saw England emerge not only as a world power, but as a superpower. Gradually, the standard of living rose and the hardships imposed by the Industrial Revolution eased under the generosity of wealthy philanthropists like Lord Shaftsbury. Evangelical preaching flourished under men like Charles

Queen Victoria Presenting the Bible

Spurgeon. But Victoria did not see this change as due to her politics or personal example, but to the role of the Bible in English culture.

When an African chief visited at the Court of St. James in London, he could not believe his eyes. He asked Queen Victoria the secret of England's greatness. Instead of taking him on a tour of the Tower of London or showing him the glittering crown jewels, Victoria picked up a Bible and handed it to the chief. "This," she said, "is the secret of England's greatness."

There is an anecdote that Queen Victoria presented a prince from India with a Bible. His response showed that he recognized that it was obeying the Bible that had made England great. The following is his attributed response.

"Where did the English-speaking people get all their intelligence and energy and cleverness and power? It is their Bible that gives it to them. And now they bring it to us and say, 'This is what raised us. Take it and raise yourselves.' "

Queen Victoria demonstrated virtue throughout her long and honorable reign.

That book [The Bible] accounts for the supremacy of England.

—Queen Victoria

Questions

1. Tell of the experience which saved Victoria's life when she was eighteen years old.
2. To what did Victoria attribute the rescue?
3. Tell of another instance when her life was providentially saved.
4. What did Queen Victoria determine when she became queen?
5. How did this affect the entire country?
6. What did Queen Victoria say was the secret of England's success while speaking to the African chief?
7. What was her statement to the prince from India?
8. How did Queen Victoria demonstrate virtue in her reign over England?

Wisdom

DEFINITION

Learning to see life from
God's point of view

MEMORY VERSE

So teach us to number our days,
that we may apply our hearts unto
wisdom.
Psalm 90:12

Matthew Fontaine Maury

Sea Path

Washington, D.C.

1842

The round white dome of the United States Naval Observatory loomed up behind him. Superintendent Matthew Fontaine Maury picked up a weighted bottle and threw it into the Potomac River. The tide was going slow, and as the current caught the "drift bottle," it spun and bobbed just below the surface. Sealed inside the bottle, a wad of paper instructed the person who found a bottle washed ashore to return it. It seemed like a child's game, setting bottles adrift at sea, or the desperate voice of a castaway on a desert island. Maury tossed another. He leaned closer to watch, the foggy air rising from the swampy Potomac mud flats dampening the wispy dark hair on his broad forehead. It happened again. The wind did not touch the bottles. He watched them drift away from the shore, following the mysterious pattern of currents.

"The paths of the seas." The words from Psalm 8 stuck in his mind. As a Christian, Maury knew that the Bible was specific: if it spoke of creatures swimming along paths, it must mean that the sea had literal paths, not just figurative ones. And actual paths could be charted.

Weeks passed. He waited for a message from beyond the Observatory. Then the bottles started coming back. People picked them up along the mud banks or lonely stretches of shoreline. They had dates and locations. Maury began digging through dusty, abandoned trunks and sea chests at the Naval Observatory. Shivering with excitement, he uncovered a vast collection of thousands of ships' logbooks and charts. The thick pages, stained from the years, dated back to the start of the United States Navy with the Maritime Committee of 1775. A great idea came to his mind.

He had always loved the sea: its mystery, its magnetic pull. Sailors relied on trade winds to buoy their vessels across the ocean. A contrary wind could drive a ship hundreds of miles off course to founder in low tides. A lack of wind could "becalm" ship and

Matthew Fontaine Maury

crew in waters as smooth as glass for days or weeks. Whalers sailed out blindly to hunt sea mammals, often for years, not realizing that whales migrated across the sea in a regular pattern. If Maury discovered these routes, mariners could trace the depths of the sea as easily as a man studies a land map. Scanning the ships' logs, he found that the old captains had often noted the way winds and currents affected a vessel. Hidden away in storage, everyone had forgotten these lessons.

Maury brought these studies to life. He made practical experiments such as the "drift bottles." His calculations told him where the currents had carried the bottles to and how long it had taken them to reach there. With a team of trained officers and men, he studied the stars and made weather forecasts. By the early 1850s, he had drawn the first accurate charts showing the bottom of the Atlantic Ocean between the United States and Europe.

Maury believed that communication was vital to exchanging new information. He pioneered the idea of laying undersea cables across the Atlantic to Europe. In the days before the telegraph, such an idea was both practical and revolutionary. One person could not encompass the wealth of human experience. By sharing with other nations, America would not only add to its own knowledge of science, but also set the United States on the road to working closely with international governments. Interested in expeditions and railways, Matthew Maury sponsored a mission to the interior of the Amazon and a railroad over the Isthmus of Panama.

Then in the spring of 1861, Maury's naval career came to an end. His home state, Virginia, seceded from the Union and the United States burst into war. Now 55 years old, Matthew Maury resigned from his post at the United States Naval Observatory and moved home.

During the war, Maury put his genius to good use. Sent to England and France to obtain ships and supplies for the Confederacy, which was hemmed in by the Union blockade of the southern coast, Maury spoke out through speeches and articles, calling for an end to war. But his convictions did not stop Maury from developing an electric torpedo. From his work with Samuel F. B. Morse, Maury knew how to work with transatlantic cable and a current of electricity flowing through underwater wires. Exploding among Yankee ships, much like a modern contact mine, Maury's deadly invention caused so much damage to northern shipping that the Secretary of the Navy complained the electric torpedo had cost the Union more ships than all other causes put together.

When the Civil War ended, Maury began to teach physics at the Virginia Military Institute in Lexington,

Virginia. Living in the same town as Confederate General Robert E. Lee, Maury served as one of the pall-bearers at Lee's funeral. After his discovery of the "paths through the seas," Maury published over 20 books and articles on how to make the seas safer for sailors. His *Physical Geography of the Sea* was the first textbook of modern oceanography. Edited from outdated diagrams, his books became the guide for all pilot charts distributed by the government to military and merchant mariners. Most importantly, Maury gave practical advice to shipmasters how to cut down on the time and expense of a voyage. By taking direct routes and avoiding costly delays, captains could now ship goods faster and to greater profit.

Today, the Virginia Military Institute Museum contains a glass display case dedicated to the work of Matthew Maury. Inside are displayed photographs, maps, and instruments that depict how Maury plotted the paths through the seas. Beside the Matthew Maury Highway that runs through Goshen Pass, a statue of the officer and scientist stands in tribute to the "Pathfinder of the Seas."

Matthew Maury showed wisdom by using biblical precepts and the resources he had at hand to plot the currents through the sea in order to make voyages safer for sailors and ships.

And as for the general system of atmospherical circulation which I have so long been endeavouring to describe, the Bible tells all in a single sentence: "The wind goeth towards the south, and turneth about unto the north; it whirleth about continually, and the wind returneth again according to his circuits." Eccl. 1:6

—Matthew Fontaine Maury, in his book, The Physical Geography of the Sea

Questions

1. What verse in Scripture caused Matthew Maury to contemplate the paths of the sea?
2. Tell what practical plan he put into place to investigate this further.
3. What idea did he pioneer?
4. What did Matthew Maury do during the Civil War?
5. What did he do after the Civil War?
6. What practical advice was he able to give to shipmasters?
7. How did Maury use biblical wisdom to benefit others?

Initiative

DEFINITION

Seeing a need and taking
responsibility to meet
it without being asked

MEMORY VERSE

Whatsoever thy hand findeth to do,
do it with thy might.
Ecclesiastes 9:10a

General in Disguise

Colonel John Hunt Morgan

Lebanon, Kentucky

Spring 1862

Lebanon, Kentucky: Spring, 1862. "Click-click! Click-click!" In the little telegraph office, the Union operator crouched over his desk, his fingers racing as he typed the dispatch from Louisville to Nashville. Soldiers in blue coats patrolled the town, waiting for something to happen. A few minutes ago, a telegram had come in, ordering Don Carlos Buell's Federal Army of the Ohio to transfer the recently captured Confederate prisoners from Colonel John Hunt Morgan's regiment to Nashville for safety. The Union

Army at Louisville expected trouble. Determined to get his men back, Morgan might attack at any time. A chill ran down the civilian operator's spine.

He muttered: "Who knows, but that guerilla may pounce like a hawk on me, too. If I only had him here, wouldn't I put an end to his villainy!"

Horses' hooves clopped in the road outside. The operator rushed to the window to look out. A tall, broad-shouldered man wearing a butternut suit had just dismounted from his horse. He wore a clustering auburn beard and mustache. Soft auburn hair curled from beneath the torn brim of a shabby slouch hat. He deftly tied his horse's bridle to a fence near the door. A moment later, his shadow darkened the office floor. Chocolate-colored Kentucky mud spattered his coat and boots. Walking slowly over to an empty chair, he sat down.

"What news?" he asked, casually.

"No news." The operator's voice was curt. He smothered a yawn and turned back to his instrument.

Grasping his riding whip in one hand, the stranger picked up the Louisville morning journal lying on the desk. Opening it, he glanced down the first column and lifted his eyebrows.

"John Morgan at work again!" he murmured. "A pity that man can't be caught."

The telegraph operator could not keep quiet. The indignation that had been seething inside of him all morning since he read the telegram boiled over. He leapt to his feet. Pacing back and forth across the room, he burst out:

"Yes, the scoundrel, the villain! If I had him here, I would soon put a ball through his cursed body. No more pranks from him, the mighty John Morgan, I tell you!"

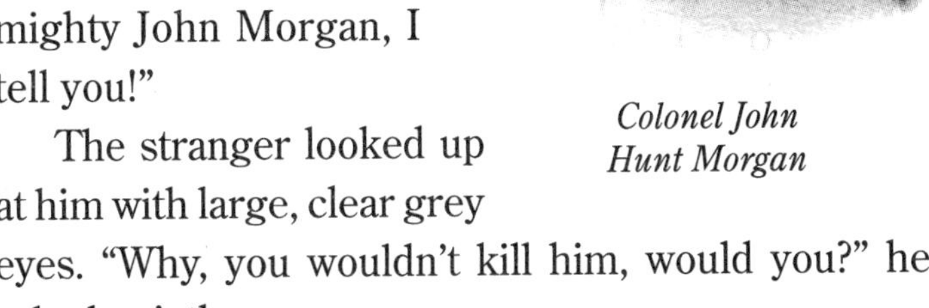

Colonel John Hunt Morgan

The stranger looked up at him with large, clear grey eyes. "Why, you wouldn't kill him, would you?" he asked quietly.

The operator clenched and swung his fist.

"Kill him? Aye, that I would, sooner than I'd shoot a mad dog. I just dare him, at any time, to cross that door, and if he isn't a dead man in five minutes, there's no truth in me!"

The man slid the folded paper across the desk. Then he rose, swept off his hat and stepped up to the operator. Slipping his hand into his hip pocket, he held out a pistol in front of him.

His soft, musical voice was gentle. "I am John Morgan, sir. Now execute your threat. Here is a pistol; you are entirely welcome to use it."

The gun lying on the outstretched palm did not falter.

The operator turned white. But Colonel Morgan stared at him with intense grey eyes. Trembling from head to foot, the operator began backing away.

"I, I—didn't know—I hadn't any idea—that you were Colonel Morgan, Sir—indeed, Sir, I didn't—I beg pardon, Sir, ten thousand times, Sir."

His voice shook. He kept edging away, holding out his hands, until his back struck against the wall. All the time, he kept babbling incoherently.

"You have my pardon, Sir." Morgan's voice was firm now. "Another time, I would advise you to be less boastful of your courage and veracity."

Then his voice changed. It turned sharp like a winter wind whistling through Cumberland Gap. "Be quick. Seat yourself and send the messages that I shall dictate to Louisville."

Morgan stood behind the operator with a pistol as he quickly slid into his chair. "Make no mistake," Morgan warned him. "If you do, your life is the forfeit. I understand the operation, Sir; therefore, don't attempt to give any information but what I instruct you."

The messages winged on their way under the operator's fingers. As he finished, Morgan demanded, "Now, show me all the dispatches that have passed through this office in the last 24 hours."

Lebanon was full of Union troops. But the operator could not alert them or cry out for help without risking a shot in the back of the head. Slowly, he pushed the stack of messages towards Morgan. The

Colonel scanned them carefully, his eyes flashing up and down the pages. At last, he laid them down. Pushing his slouched hat back on his head, he walked to the door.

"That will do, Sir," he called over his shoulder. "Good morning." Striding to his horse, he sprang into the saddle and galloped away.

During Union General Edward McCook's occupation of Nashville, Morgan struck on a plan to lure a large number of Union troops into an ambush. Dressed in a homespun coat and trousers, he climbed into a farmer's wagon and drove into Nashville. Bags of meal bought from a local miller bounced behind him. Morgan stopped in front of the hotel where General McCook always ate his meals. Leaving his assistant to watch the horse, Morgan sauntered into the hotel. He sniffed the air and stared at the menu, but all the time, his eyes darted around the room.

General Edward McCook

Suddenly, he spotted General McCook, with long mustaches and thinning dark hair, sitting at a table across the room. The farmer shambled up to the table and fell into a chair.

"Is this heah Gineral McCook?" he drawled.

The General smiled pleasantly up from his meal. "That's my name."

"Wal, Gineral," the lazy tones droned, "if thar's no Secesh 'bout, I've got sum'pen ter tell you right heah." He dropped his voice. "I live up close by Burk's Mills in the middle of a nest of red hot Seceshers and they swar' yer sojers shant hev a speck o' meal if they starve for it." A grin spread across his face. "But Gineral, I got a wagon load of meal ground, and I hev' brung it down heah ter day, and it's now out thar in the street and you kin hev it if you want it."

General McCook, touched by the man's loyalty and generosity, smiled his thanks warmly. But he could not take a farmer's hard-earned flour without any payment. "Take the meal, my friend, to the Commissary," he offered kindly. "He will pay you for it in gold and silver."

Morgan tucked into his dinner with an appetite. When he had cleaned his plate, he lurched out of his chair, bumped the table and gave a clumsy little bow. Dragging his feet, he left the room. Half an hour later, he went down to Federal Headquarters. A staff officer assured the farmer that McCook was in. Morgan shambled up to the General with sleeve-plucking eagerness.

"Gineral—" His voice was anxious—"Can't yer send 150 men up thar to the neberhood of Burk's Mills? I'll guide 'em into that nest er traitors and secheshers; and they kin capture too a mighty big sight er meal."

General McCook could not thank this patriot enough. "The men, my friend, shall certainly be sent. Which day shall we choose? Let the appointment be as early as possible." He paused impressively. "I suppose this is a busy time with you farmers, but when one's country calls, the plough itself must stop in the furrow."

Morgan agreed. He protested loudly that his farm could fall to pieces before he would allow one Secessionist to escape. Then he set the date and time for the meeting.

A few days later, 150 Union cavalrymen trotted out to the lonely place to meet up with the Kentucky farmer. Instead, they came face to face with Morgan surrounded by more than a company of Confederate raiders. The astonished soldiers surrendered on the spot.

The brother-in-law of Robert E. Lee's General Ambrose Powell Hill, John Hunt Morgan continued his raiding expeditions through Kentucky and Tennessee. In spite of his success as the "Marion of the West," there is evidence that the Confederate authorities began to investigate Morgan's activities as a bandit.

In April 1863, he crossed the Ohio River into southern Indiana and Ohio on an expedition known as "Morgan's Raid." Morgan intended to relieve

Morgan's Raiders, Prisoners-of-war in Ohio State Penitentiary

pressure on Bragg's forces currently besieged by General Rosecrans' troops.

Pushing north towards Cincinnati, Morgan escaped the pursuing Union cavalry for almost a week. After a final clash with 450 Home Guard troops while trying to cross into West Virginia at Buffington Island, Morgan found himself imprisoned in the Ohio State Penitentiary.

But Morgan did not give up. Using handmade tools, Morgan and six of his officers chipped away at a wall for twenty-three days. Then they broke through to the soft, dark earth and began digging a 100-foot tunnel. At midnight, they stuffed their flannel shirts with bed-sheets to make dummies. Then they slipped into the tunnel. Breaking out into the yard, they descended to the ground below using a rope made out of blankets and the aid of a bent iron poker. Breathing the cool night air again, the Confederates faded past the guards into the darkness. Morgan made his way home alternately by foot, wagon, and train.

General John Hunt Morgan demonstrated initiative by inventing ways out of difficult situations and employing methods of disguise to achieve victory over enemy forces.

"When he died, the glory and chivalry seemed gone from the struggle, and it became a tedious routine, enjoined by duty, and sustained only by sentiments of pride and hatred. Surely men never grieved for a leader as Morgan's men sorrowed for him. The tears which scalded the cheeks of hardy and rugged veterans, who had witnessed all the terrible scenes of four years of war, attested it, and the sad faces told of the aching hearts within."

—from History of Morgan's Calvary (1867)

Questions

1. Why were the Union soldiers on edge?
2. What threats toward John Morgan did the telegraph operator make?
3. What happened to shock him?
4. What did John Morgan command him to do?
5. How did Morgan lure Union troops into an ambush in Nashville?
6. Tell how Morgan and his men made their escape from prison.
7. Give several examples of initiative in John Morgan's life.

Gentleness

DEFINITION

Responding to others in a kind, understanding manner

MEMORY VERSE

And the servant of the Lord
must not strive;
but be gentle unto all men,
apt to teach, patient.
2 Timothy 2:24

After the Battle

President Abraham Lincoln

Washington, D.C.
September 1862

Washington: September 1862. His steps slowed as he entered the Navy yard. The sinking sun glinted off the iron hulks of ships lying belly-deep in the Anacostia River, on the yellow curls of wood shavings under his feet. Near the Eastern Market on Pennsylvania Avenue and 9th Street, the grim, dirty windows of the naval hospital loomed up before him like a brick prison. Leaves were beginning to fall somewhere in the city—crimson, golden, brown. How many hospitals had he visited today? Thirty? Forty? After walking the halls of Georgetown University Hospital at dawn, he had lost count. There were hospitals in homes, hotels, schools, and churches, on Capitol Hill, in the Patent Office, the Armory Square building and Camp Alexander, even in wooden shacks. A city of 75,000 civilians found 50,000 wounded crowding their doors. Moving from east to west, he had tried to visit every hospital in the city.

They were waiting for him as he walked up the broad steps.

"This way, Mr. President."

He never let them announce his name. He appeared in the high-ceilinged ward, moving slowly, his long black frock coat swaying against his knees. They lay in rows, without words, their eyes turned towards him. He grasped their hands, his tenor voice a blend of Indiana and Kentucky bluegrass. They are children. Some of them almost babies. Their shirts were open at the throat, their eyes fixed on him.

Old Naval Hospital, Washington, D.C.

"My brave boys. Some had old eyes, eyes that had seen Union victories and defeats at Shiloh, Bull Run, Antietam. God, this war. What are we doing? How can we love and hate at the same time? Why are we fighting? For what?"

He knew the answer. So that thousands of men, women, and children could live free. So that the freedom they died for would not be in vain. But looking at their faces, he forgot them—forgot that the boys lying here in their grey coats were enemies.

President Abraham Lincoln

"Do they know that I don't hate them? That I never wanted this war? But they will say I did, that I pushed the country into this."

He moved along, touching their bedclothes, saying a few words, trying to infuse his strength into them as he passed. "I can't stay, boys," he said. "I hope you are all comfortable and getting along nicely here."

The face stared up at him from the cot. A thin, white face. Almost a child. He could see bandaged limbs, the loose grey Confederate coat, the body making barely a ripple under the blanket. "What are you doing here? Why did they let you go?" The eyes looked up at him without fear. Trusting. He paused by the cot for a moment, closed his eyes in prayer. "What more can I do?"

His carriage was waiting in the yard, black as a funeral hearse. Nearby came the sound of lapping water. He put his square-toed boot on the step, and reached to pull himself in. Suddenly, a woman's voice called out. He looked back. A nurse came running towards him.

"Please, Mr. Lincoln. The dying Confederate boy wants to see you again."

It was time to go home now. Home to Mary's dark face, stacks of papers from the War Office, critical newsmen, and gloomy cabinet ministers, then dinner, lying on the carpet while the children hauled a goat and cart through the library. Weariness sucked at his bones, weighing him down. But he was in the race. He could not give up when so many depended on him. A smile creased his tired face, lighting up the dark hollows of his eyes. It shone softly through the gaunt cheeks like a light through an alabaster vase.

President Abraham Lincoln

"I'll go."

They were lighting the lamps as he entered the ward. The face was a little greyer now, the shadows bluish.

"What can I do for you?"

He saw the pleading in the boy's eyes.

"I am so lonely and friendless, Mr. Lincoln"—the voice came in a whisper—"and I am hoping that you can tell me what my mother would want me to say and do now."

If only those big, gnarled hands, scarred from years

of chopping forests, could reach out and envelop all these boys. His boys. "My concern is not whether God is on our side," he once said. "My greatest concern is to be on God's side, for God is always right."

He knelt in the yellow lamplight. "Yes, my boy. I know exactly what your mother would want you to say and do. And I am glad that you sent for me to come back to you. I can pray, now. I have learned to pray since this war, since my boy Willie died.

"Now, as I kneel here, please repeat the words after me." The sun dropped lower in the western sky, gilding the high windowpanes and falling on the young face. He cradled the boy's head on his arm, easing those last moments with his own strength as he whispered the words.

Now I lay me down to sleep:
I pray the Lord my soul to keep.
If I should die before I wake,
I pray the Lord my soul to take.
And this I ask for Jesus' sake.

It was a simple prayer, one that his mother had taught him. A prayer spoken between friends. A nighttime prayer to end the day.

Abraham Lincoln showed gentleness towards the captured Confederate soldier. Rather than seeing just another prisoner, Lincoln saw a lonely boy who needed prayer and assurance as he prepared for his final journey.

Near eighty years ago we began by declaring that all men are created equal; but now from that beginning we have run down to the other declaration, that for SOME men to enslave OTHERS is a "sacred right of self-government." These principles can not stand together. They are as opposite as God and mammon; and whoever holds to the one, must despise the other.

—Abraham Lincoln, October 16, 1854,
a speech at Peoria, Illinois

Questions

1. What was President Lincoln doing?
2. How many wounded were the townspeople caring for?
3. Why did he go back into the hospital after leaving?
4. How did he show gentleness to the young Confederate boy?
5. What did the boy request?
6. How did Lincoln answer him?
7. To whom do you have the opportunity to show gentleness?

Boldness

DEFINITION

Facing confrontation with the assurance
that God will bless the outcome
if I'm standing firm for truth

MEMORY VERSE

The rich man is wise in his own conceit;
but the poor that hath understanding
searcheth him out.
Proverbs 28:11

Featherbed Raid

Captain John S. Mosby

Virginia

March 1863

Midnight: Sunday, March 8, 1863. A light rain sprinkled the gum capes of the twenty-nine grey-clad men waiting on the Little River turnpike. They glanced at each other furtively. No one knew what game was afoot tonight. Sitting his horse under the canopy of trees, Captain John S. Mosby leaned forward eagerly. Cold drops bounced off the brim of his grey slouch hat. It was hard to see Mosby in the darkness. He was the color of the night, earth-tones and rain.

Captain John S. Mosby

"Big Yankee" Ames, a deserter from the Fifth New York Cavalry, sidled close to Mosby's saddle. Ames had come to the Confederates from Union lines, and now he was leading them back again. When the Union pickets pulled back that night, they had left a gap in the line between Centerville and Chantilly. That gap was still open. Better still, General Stoughton had set up headquarters apart from his men at Fairfax Court House. It was too good a chance to miss.

Mosby felt his heart contract. If the raid didn't come off, he could kiss goodbye to his military career. The Rangers slid out onto the Little River pike. For almost an hour, there was only the pounding of hoofbeats. All at once, Mosby veered off the main road. Whippoorwills called softly; rabbits sprang from under the horses' hooves. Weaving in and out among the pines, they breached the gap in the line and plunged on the first guards like jackrabbits, capturing every man alive. Wheeling onto the Warrenton pike, they approached Fairfax from the railroad station.

It was now 2 a.m. Most of the Rangers split off to the Provost Marshal's stables, silencing the guards and hustling out the horses. Meanwhile, Mosby and five men struck through town. It was hard to see in the slanting rain. Just west of the courthouse on Main Street, Mosby's men reached Stoughton's headquarters, a two-story brick house with white trim belonging to Dr. William P. Gunnel. A window crashed open on the second floor.

"Who's there?" an officer called.

Mosby threw back his head. "Fifth New York Cavalry with a dispatch for General Stoughton."

The Rangers rode up, surrounded the porch. Lieutenant Prentiss stood there in his nightshirt, stretching out his hand for the dispatch. Mosby seized the man by the collar.

"Take me to General Stoughton's room."

Prentiss had no choice. With Mosby close behind him, he mounted the stairs. The door creaked open. In the dim, smoky light, Mosby saw Stoughton lying in bed, his face turned to the wall. Leaning over him, Mosby jerked the covers down and slapped Stoughton's bare back.

"Is this General Stoughton?" he barked.

Stoughton opened his eyes. In the glare of the lamp, three men were pointing pistols at his face. "Yes, what do you want?"

"Do you know Mosby, General?"

"Yes! Have you caught the rascal?" Stoughton grunted.

"No, but he has caught you!"

Mosby's high-pitched, powerful voice continued. "Jackson is at Centerville and Stuart is in possession of all your camps. You may have heard of Captain Mosby. I am Mosby."

General Edwin Stoughton

Stoughton stared at him. "Oh, yes, I have heard of him, but Jackson is not at Centerville, nor could Stuart be in possession of the camps about here without my hearing of it. I think you are a raiding party and a small one, at that. Is Fitz here?"

Mosby nodded. "Yes."

"Well, take me to him. We were classmates."

"Certainly, but be quick."

Stoughton began to pull on his clothes. Stooping to the fireplace, Mosby picked up a piece of charcoal and scrawled his name on the wall "Mosby." Main Street was full of Rangers herding prisoners together. Rain was still falling, the snorting horses churning the melting snow to slush underfoot. As the cavalry clattered past the courthouse, Stoughton, soaked to the skin, remarked:

"This is a bold thing you have done, but you will certainly be caught."

"Perhaps so." Mosby's voice was soft as rain.

As Mosby's Rangers melted into the woods like smoke, less than one hundred yards from the Union pickets, the main body of the Federal Army had no idea of the raid. In one bold stroke, Mosby had captured the youngest general in the Union Army, 32 men and 58 horses. It was an act that was to establish John S. Mosby's reputation for the rest of the war.

The wicked flee when no man pursueth: but the righteous are bold as a lion.

—Proverbs 28:1

Questions

1. What act of boldness did Mosby perform in this story?
2. How did it demonstrate boldness?
3. What did he accomplish by his bold action?
4. How did Mosby's men work together to accomplish this achievement?
5. What did Mosby risk if his plan failed?
6. In what situations in your life do you need to demonstrate boldness?
7. Think of a situation you have encountered that boldness would help accomplish godly purposes. How might you show boldness now?

Sensitivity

DEFINITION

The ability to put yourself in another's shoes and trying to see life from his point of view

MEMORY VERSE

Put on therefore, as the elect of God, holy and beloved, bowels of mercies, kindness, humbleness of mind, meekness, long-suffering; Forbearing one another . . .

Colossians 3:12-13a

Blue and Grey

General Robert E. Lee

Gettysburg, Pennsylvania

July 1863

Gettysburg: July 3, 1863. When he opened his eyes, he could see smoke drifting like grey cotton wool around the shattered trees atop Cemetery Ridge. Marcus Wright, lying on his back, tried to shift onto his side. *What is the matter with me?* His blue coat smelled of blood and sweat. He remembered running across the field, wavering like a mist in the bright sunshine. Suddenly, his left leg went down as if it had plunged into a rabbit hole. He knew what hit him. A *Minié* ball.

General Robert E. Lee

It was morning when Wright came across this field, young, strong. Dew drops clung to the stalks of grass not yet trampled by the men swinging haversacks and rifles. The sun started to go down. A sad orange light spread across the fields, turning the dark smudge of woods into a heart of darkness. Nothing existed before this pain. Nothing would exist after. Pain and the heat on his forehead, these were the enemies he had to contend with now. The others were out of his reach.

Bitterness rose in Wright's throat. Just to move. An inch. It was torture to lie still while the bleak heights loomed above him like an overturned bowl and the trees walked upside-down over his head. He didn't know how long he lay there. Only that his leg was shattered like a glass figurine.

"Kill them. Kill them." The words beat about in his brain, multiplied by feverish pain and the vicious flies buzzing around his face. The Confederates were animals. They didn't deserve to live. His anger flared to a hundred degrees. If he could see one of them right now, he'd shoot them down like dogs. But he couldn't move. Couldn't move.

The sound of hooves. Voices muttering. Southern voices, a drawl. Then Wright saw them. They were riding under the shadows of Cemetery Ridge, grey men on grey horses. He focused on the nearest one with the soiled white gauntlets, grey slouch hat, three gold stars sewn onto the lapel. Wright recognized him from his war photographs.

General Robert E. Lee.

They were going by him, getting away. The blood swam to his head. Marcus lifted his hands high, staring straight into Lee's face. His lips, cracked with thirst, spread in a grimace.

"Hurrah for the Union!" he yelled.

There was silence. Then the man dismounted, came towards him. He could see his tall black jackboots heading for his face.

"Lee is going to kill me," Wright thought to himself.

The boots stopped right by his head. He looked up into a tired face, the eyes so sad that he had to look away. This man was human. The winged hair under the slouched hat was nearly white. Marcus felt the fear draining out of him, seeping into the flowers, the grass, the earth. Why did his eyes look like that, so gentle? What was he going to do? Then General Lee reached down and firmly squeezed his hot, heavy hand.

"My son," Lee said quietly, "I hope you will soon be well."

Deep brown eyes stared into his. Wright thought to himself. He could see the fine, tired lines around them, puffy dark pouches from sleepless nights, the skin burned brown by the sun. Looking into Lee's face, Wright felt the slow punishment of defeat, the death of one-third of his general officers, the winding path towards the Potomac. Slowly, the hand released his. He wanted to keep looking, to remember that face as long as he lived. Then he was gone, out of his life forever.

Hot tears welled up in Wright's eyes. "I taunted Lee as he passed by. I wanted to hurt him, to make him feel the pain I was feeling. And he felt it. But not as I thought. I was an enemy, and he stopped to comfort me. He took the pain for me."

The stars came out. And the boy lay on his back in the bloody grass, tears wet on his cheeks, tears of loneliness, repentance, and love.

Instead of taking the insult personally, Robert E. Lee was able to put himself in his enemy's shoes and show sensitivity towards the wounded Union soldier.

A true man of honor feels humbled himself when he cannot help humbling others.

Do your duty in all things. You cannot do more, you should never wish to do less.

—General Robert E. Lee

Questions

1. What feeling did this wounded Yankee soldier have for all Confederates?
2. Bitterness is a poison that clouds the way we see reality. It wants to hurt others and get revenge. How did bitterness affect Marcus Wright?
3. What changed the boy's attitude?
4. What can you tell of the character of Robert E. Lee by the way he treated Wright?
5. How deeply did this encounter affect the way Wright thought?
6. When others mistreat us, the natural reaction is to mistreat them back. Explain how God can work His purposes when one person purposes to do right.
7. If Wright lived, how do you think his life was most likely changed by this encounter?
8. Think of an instance when someone mistreated you. How did you respond? What was the reaction of the person who offended you? If you reacted wrongly, how should you have acted?
9. Will you determine to be that person who seeks to do right even when treated wrongly by others?

Tolerance

DEFINITION

Giving others room to
grow at different
rates as God leads them.

MEMORY VERSE

But when ye sin so against the
brethren, and wound their weak
conscience, ye sin against Christ.
Wherefore, if meat make my
brother to offend, I will eat no
flesh while the world standeth, lest
I make my brother to offend.

1 Corinthians 8:12–13

God's Army

William Booth

East End, London

1865

He staggered through a squalid labyrinth of twisting streets. Muck slid underfoot. The smell of gin stung his nostrils. Behind him, William Booth heard a yell in the darkness. A stone struck his head. Blood ran down the side of his face, clotting in his beard. Filthy dens crouched on every corner, where 290 people packed into a single acre. Behind the dim shutters, bottles crashed and small children climbed steps to reach the counter for a glass of gin. Tonight, a crowd of roughs had smashed the glass and threw fireworks through the windows of the Christian Mission warehouse where Booth and a group of worshippers huddled in the flickering light of naphtha flares. All day, Booth, his wife Catherine, and a handful of Christian workers dished out soup in their "Food for the Million" kitchens and visited the sick and a few converts.

Day and night, he preached repentance from sin through faith in Jesus Christ. Tonight, as on many past nights, he stumbled through the East End lanes, pursued by a gang of drunken roughs known as the "Skeleton Army." But still he went on. Exhausted, his clothes torn and a bloody bandage wrapped around his head, Booth stumbled home.

"Go for souls and go for the worst!" he maintained.

He would never give up. He had come to London's East End as a thirty-six-year-old preacher, intent on winning the lost and poor to Christ. At a time in the nineteenth century when missionaries flooded overseas to mission fields in China, Africa, and India, Booth never even left London. "I seemed to hear a voice sounding in my ears," he said, "Where can you go and find such heathen as these, and where is there so great a need for your labors?"

At age fifteen, after attending a Methodist prayer meeting, Booth wrote in his diary: "God shall have all there is of William Booth." Born into poverty, he would work among the poor all of his life, eventually winning the title, "The Prophet of the Poor."

Salvation Army General William Booth

Booth initially held open-air meetings in haylofts, in the crowded backrooms of a pigeon shop, and in the old Quaker burial wasteland near Whitechapel. He used lively music to attract a crowd and then delivered a short message, exhorting them to come to Christ.

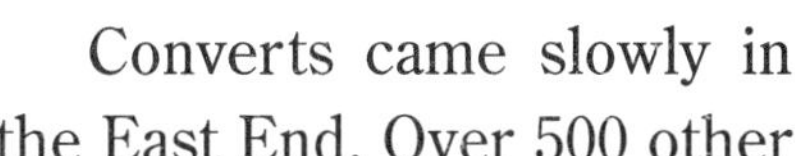

Converts came slowly in the East End. Over 500 other religious and social groups besides Booth's organization existed throughout the city. But the people were hard to win. Booth believed that Christian ministers should demonstrate their faith by "loosing the chains of injustice, freeing the captive and oppressed, sharing food and home, clothing the naked, and carrying out family responsibilities." Booth's wife Catherine was outspoken in her belief in the need for reform. Practical Christianity, she argued, should better society.

This belief extended to the Booths' children. Rather than shielding them from life in the East End slums, William and Catherine involved their children in feeding, clothing, and preaching to the poor from a young age. They saw hooligans throw stones at their father and aristocrats such as Lord Shaftsbury criticize their mother for speaking in public. They learned to condemn sin while loving the drunkards, unwed mothers, and homeless children caught up in it.

One day in 1868, as Booth dictated a letter to his secretary George Railton, he referred to their organization as a "volunteer army." His son Bramwell looked up and exclaimed: "Volunteer! I'm no volunteer, I'm a regular!"

George Railton

Booth immediately ordered Railton to cross out the word "volunteer" and substitute the word "salvation." The Salvation Army was born. Booth became its "general," longstanding members became its "officers," and the rest of the workers held the rank of "soldier." The Army invented its own flags, uniforms, and stirring Christian songs based on popular folk tunes. Booth held informal services to encourage new believers with singing, instrumental accompaniments, handclapping, and sermons. When outsiders criticized him for using secular tunes to attract crowds, Booth shot back: "Secular music, do you say, belongs to the Devil? Does it? Well, if it did I would plunder him for it, for he has no right to a single note of the whole seven."

Money dribbled in slowly. Many of the volunteers were women, who worked hard alongside the men. They made such an impact in his slum ministry that Booth once exclaimed: "My best men are women!"

Booth continued under increasing hostility from the Church of England, who looked down on his radical activities. Lord Shaftsbury even denounced Booth as the "Anti-Christ." Members of the Salvation Army faced imprisonment for holding open-air meetings and endured harassment by the "Skeleton Army" for their condemnation of alcohol.

William and Catherine Booth also campaigned for improving the conditions of working women at the large Bryant and May factory in the East End. In the days before labor laws protected workers or limited hours, these women earned a little over one shilling during a grueling 16-hour day. They repeatedly dipped match-heads in poisonous yellow phosphorus. Exposed to the deadly fumes, the skin on the side of their faces turned green and then black. In the final stages of "Phossy Jaw," the bone simply rotted away, causing a painful death.

The Booths tried to get the manufacturers to use harmless red phosphorus instead of the hazardous yellow, as many other countries did. But Bryant and May fought back, arguing that red phosphorus cost more. Customers would not pay such a high price for matches.

Unable to improve Bryant and May's working conditions, Booth opened his own match factory in Old Ford, East End, in 1891. Under these healthier conditions, his workers produced six million boxes of matches per year. He also paid them four-pence per day, twice the amount that Bryant and May paid their employees. As interest in the Salvation Army's work grew, Booth escorted journalists and members of Parliament around his model factory. He also showed them the miserable sweatshops where workers toiled for masters like Bryant and May. Under the pressure of bad publicity, Bryant and May finally stopped using yellow phosphorus in 1901.

An Early Salvation Army Band in the U.S.A.

Gradually, public opinion turned in favor of the Salvation Army. William Booth finally established branches of the Army in 58 countries. During his later years, he wrote, traveled, and held "salvation meetings." Emperors, kings, and presidents received him in audience and supported his work. Upon his death, ten thousand workers and William and Catherine Booth's nine children continued to carry on the work that they had begun. It still exists today.

William and Catherine Booth demonstrated genuine tolerance by loving the people they worked for in spite of abuse and persecution.

You cannot warm the hearts of people with God's love if they have an empty stomach and cold feet.

—William Booth

Questions

1. What type of people was William Booth preaching to?
2. What types of reception did he often get?
3. What title was he given?
4. How did Booth believe Christian ministers should demonstrate their faith?
5. How did the Booths train their children to tolerate the sinners but not their sin?
6. Tell how the Salvation Army got its name.
7. What became of Booth's children after his death?
8. Explain how the Booths demonstrated tolerance in the true sense of the word.

Orderliness

DEFINITION

Managing my life and my belongings in order to reach maximum potential

MEMORY VERSE

Let all things be done decently and in order.

1 Corinthians 14:40

Confederate April

Colonel Charles Marshall

Appomattox Court House
April 9, 1865

During the night, the sound of horses gnawing the bark from the trees kept Colonel Charles Marshall awake. The April wind was chilly and Marshall pulled his cape over his head to muffle the noise. But nothing could shut out the sounds of hunger. After a late-night council of war, Robert E. Lee's secretary lay in the dense wood without a blanket or tent. As Lee's adjutant from 1862 to 1865, Marshall's meticulous clerical work, his careful record-keeping, and drafting of hundreds of letters, dispatches, and general orders had earned him a high place of responsibility on Lee's staff.

Suddenly Marshall sat up, listening intently. It was 1 a.m. A column of infantry was moving along the road. Had Grant's troops spotted them? Then Marshall heard hoarse voices chanting out of the dusk. It was Hood's Texas brigade straggling along in the pre-dawn darkness, their feet aching and their stomachs empty. Headquarters broke camp as Marshall buttoned on his coat, blind without the thick spectacles he wore even in sleep.

Sunday, April 9th, 1865, dawned. As Marshall mounted his horse, the guns booming in the distance told him that General Gordon was trying to break out of the encirclement. But Union cavalry greeted his exhausted attack, forcing him back on Appomattox. Longstreet's division was in tatters, stragglers stretching out for miles. Yesterday, Lee received a note from General Grant, suggesting they discuss surrender. Now Lee told Marshall: "Write to General Grant." Throughout the morning, Marshall transmitted half a dozen notes between Grant and Lee. Both parties were dancing around the issue of surrender, Grant pushing for capitulation and Lee resisting. It was now almost noon. No further word had come from Grant. The officers climbed the slope overlooking Appomattox Court House. Lee was visibly flagging, his face showing unbearable strain. An hour passed before a white flag of truce rippled towards them. Lee rose to greet the Union officers. He was ready to meet Grant. Valuing Marshall's orderly writing, Lee asked him to accompany him. Marshall was in a "dilapidated" state. His uniform was in tatters, his gauntlets nonexistent; he had to borrow a sword. Marshall's job was to find a suitable place for the generals to meet. Soon he located a two-story brick house belonging to Wilmer McLean.

Colonel Charles Marshall with General Robert E. Lee, Signing Terms of Surrender Ending the Civil War

A short time later, Lee entered the front room, wearing snowy gauntlets and a crisp grey uniform. Marshall stood behind a marble-topped table near the window. The wall opposite them filled with tiptoeing Union officers. Half an hour ticked by. It was now 1:30 p.m. All at once, there was a loud clumping of boots in the hall. Grant had arrived. Marshall watched as the two men quietly shook hands. Then Lee got down to business. He agreed that surrender was necessary "to prevent further bloodshed." Colonel Ely Parker, Grant's aide and a leader of the Seneca Nation, carried a little oval table over to Grant, who hunched above it, scribbling out the terms of surrender. Marshall perched on the arm of the sofa, chatting with General Sheridan as the two generals discussed the disposition of arms, baggage, and horses. They crossed out a word here, inserted a phrase there.

Glancing at the draft, Lee noticed that the surrender conditions did not allow the Confederates to keep their own animals. "That is clear."

Grant, noting the wistful tone, said hastily, "I will instruct the officers to let all the men who claim to own a horse or mule take the animals home with them to work their little farms."

Lee's face cleared. "This will have the best possible effect upon my men."

Parker went to the rear of the room and began to copy the surrender terms. But he ran out of ink. With his usual method, Marshall reached into the satchel at his side and offered Parker the boxwood inkwell he always carried with him.

Then it was Marshall's turn to draft a reply. Lee cut him short. "Don't say 'I have the honor.' Just say, 'I accept the terms.' " Sitting down, Marshall wrote in his beautiful, copperplate handwriting:

"We, the prisoners of war belonging to the Army of Northern Virginia [have] this day surrendered by General Robert E. Lee."

It was 4 p.m. Beyond the window, the fifth spring of the war was beginning. Marshall had to turn his face away, because there were tears in his eyes.

Because of his orderliness, Colonel Charles Marshall was chosen to draft the important document officially ending the Civil War in Virginia. He was one of the two Confederates present at the surrender, and the only one to later write about it.

Teach me, O LORD, the way of thy statutes; and I shall keep it unto the end.

—Psalm 119:33

Questions

1. What quality had won Col. Marshall the position of high responsibility on Robert E. Lee's staff?
2. Why was it so important to keep careful details?
3. How did Col. Marshall's orderliness in being prepared show during the surrender?
4. Why is it important as a youth to hone your skills or orderliness in preparation for your future? (Remember David in Scripture who learned to be proficient in the use of a slingshot as a boy. How did God use that in the future?)
5. What are ways you could improve in orderliness? Your room? Your belongings? Your schoolwork? Your chores? Your ministry to others?

Selected Bibliography

Andreyev, Ivan. *Russia's Catacomb Saints: Lives of the New Martyrs*. California: Saint Herman of Alaska Press, 1982.

Bashkiroff, Zenaide. *Nights Are Longest There: A Young Girl's Account of Revolution in Russia*. London: M. Spearman, 1960.

Berkin, Carol. *Revolutionary Mothers: Women in the Struggle for America's Independence*. Vintage Press, 2006.

Bruce, Philip Alexander. *Brave Deeds of Confederate Soldiers*. Harrisonburg: Sprinkle Publications, 2006.

Caldwell, Charles. *Memoirs of the Life and Campaigns of the Honorable Nathaniel Greene, Major General in the Army of the United States and Commander of the Southern Department in the War of the Revolution*. Philadelphia: Robert Desilver, printer, 1819. Reprint. Nabu Press, 2010.

Callo, Joseph. *John Paul Jones: America's First Sea Warrior.* Naval Institute Press, 2006.

Cheripko, Jan. *Caesar Rodney's Ride Eighty Miles for Freedom*. Boyd's Mill Press, 2004. (Grades 3-6).

Davis, Burke. *To Appomattox: Nine April Days, 1865*. N.Y: Rinehart & Company, 1959.

Delaplaine, Edward S. *Francis Scott Key: Life and Times*. Heritage Books, 2011.

Driggs, Laurence La Tourette. *Heroes of Aviation*. Little, Brown and Company, 1918 (Armand Pinsard).

Elliot, Elisabeth. *A Chance to Die: The Life and Legacy of Amy Carmichael*. Revell Press, 2005.

Fluckey, Eugene. *Thunder Below! The USS "Barb" Revolutionizes Submarine Warfare in World War II*. University of Illinois Press, 1997. "The Flying Panther: Captain Edward J. Simpson." *American Aviation Society*, 2011.

Fougara, Katherine Gibson. *With Custer's Cavalry*. Iyer Press, 2007.

Franklin, Benjamin. *Benjamin Franklin's Autobiography*. W.W. Norton & Company, 1986.

Franks, Norman, and Harry Dempsey. *Nieuport Aces of World War I. Osprey Aircraft of the Aces*, No. 33. Osprey Publishing, 2000 (Armand Pinsard).

Gaustad, Edwin S. *Liberty of Conscience: Roger Williams in America*. Judson Press, 1999.

________________ *Roger Williams*. New York: Oxford University Press, 2005.

Gilmer, George R. *Sketches of Some of the First Settlers of Upper Georgia, of the Cherokees, and the Author.* New York 1855, 1926, p. 90 (Reprinted in 1965 by Genealogical Publishing Co., Baltimore, and 1989 by Heritage Papers, Danielsville, Georgia).

Goodyear, Robert C. *The Real Pennsylvania Dutch American, "Molly Pitcher": A Documented History.* Author House, 2012 (Suggested reading).

Grack-Koestler, Rachel A. *Molly Pitcher: Heroine of the War for Independence*. Chelsea House Publications, 2005.

Green, Roger. *The Life and Ministry of William Booth: Founder of the Salvation Army*. Abingdon Press, 2006.

Hattersley, Roy. *Blood and Fire: The Story of William and Catherine Booth and the Salvation Army*. New York: Doubleday, 2000.

Hearn, Chester G. *Tracks in the Sea: Matthew Fontaine Maury and the Mapping of the Oceans*. International Marine Press, 2003.

Hembree, Charles R. *From Pearl Harbor to the Pulpit: The Dramatic Story of Captain Fuchida and Jacob DeShazer*. Akron: Ohio, Rex Humbard World Wide Ministry, 1975.

Hocker, Edward W. *The Fighting Parson of the American Revolution: A Biography of General Peter Muhlenberg, Lutheran Clergyman, Military Chieftain and Political Leader*. Philadelphia, PA: Edward W. Hocker, 1936.

Holt, Rackham Vincent. *George Washington Carver: An American Biography*. New York: Doubleday, 1963.

Hull, Michael D. *Peter Francisco: American Revolutionary War Hero*. *Military History Magazine*, July-August, 2006.

Kackley, Paul. "The Dead Yank Hero of Orleans Forest." *Stars and Stripes*, 25 Nov. 1959.

Kalpaschnikoff, Andrei. *A Prisoner of Trotsky's*. New York: Doubleday Page, 1920.

Kidd, Thomas S. *Patrick Henry: First Among Patriots.* Basic Books, 2011.

Knight, Lucien. *Georgia's Landmarks, Memorials, and Legends.* Penguin Publishing, 2006 (Nancy Morgan Hart).

Lewis, Meriwether. *Original Journals of the Lewis and Clark Expedition, 1804-1806.* New York: Arno Press, 1969.

Littauer, V. S. *Russian Hussar.* London: J. A. Allen, 1965.

Marks, Lara. "Sacagawea as an Evolving Symbol of American Indian Women." Dec. 16, 1998.

Marshall, Charles. *An Aide-de-Camp of Lee.* Kessinger Publishing, 2007.

Muhlenberg, Henry A. *The Life of Major-General Peter Muhlenberg, of the Revolutionary Army.* Philadelphia: Carey and Hart, 1849.

Perry, John. *Sergeant York: His Life, Legend and Legacy: The Remarkable Untold Story of Sergeant Alvin C. York.* Barnes and Noble Books, 1997.

Phelps, M. William. *Nathan Hale: The Life and Death of America's First Spy.* Thomas Dunne Books, 2008.

Polsky, Michael. *The New Martyrs of Russia.* Montreal: The Saint Job of Pochaev Brotherhood, 2002.

Ramage, James A. *Grey Ghost: The Life of Colonel John Singleton Mosby.* University of Kentucky Press, 2009.

Rappleye, Charles. *Robert Morris: Financier of the American Revolution*. New York: Simon & Schuster, 2010.

Salisbury, Gay and Laney Salisbury. *The Cruelest Miles: The Heroic Story of Dogs and Men in a Race Against an Epidemic*. New York: W. W. Norton & Company, 2005.

San Souci, Robert D. *Kate Shelley: Bound for Legend.* Dial Books for Young Readers, 1995. Scott, Jane. *A Gentleman as Well as a Whig, Caesar Rodney and the American Revolution.* University of Delaware Press, 2000.

Scott, John Thomas. "Nancy Hart: 'Too Good Not to Tell Again.' "*Georgia Women: Their Lives and Times*, vol.1. Chirhart, Ann Short, and Betty Wood, Ed. Athens: University of Georgia Press, 2009.

Silcox-Jarrett, Diane. *Heroines of the American Revolution: America's Founding Mothers.* Scholastic, Inc., 2000 (Lydia Darraugh).

Skeyhill, Tom. *Sergeant York and the Great War.* The Vision Forum, Inc., 1998.

Snow, William P. *Lee and His Generals*. New York: The Fairfax Press, 1982.

Strachey, Lytton. *Queen Victoria: An Eminent Illustrated Biography.* New York: Black Dog & Leventhal Publishers, 1998.

Summers, Julie. *The Colonel of Tamarkan: Philip Toosey and the Bridge on the River Kwai*. London: Simon & Schuster, 2005.

Thomas, Evan. *John Paul Jones: Sailor, Hero, Father of the American Navy*. New York: Simon & Schuster, 2003.

Vaughan, David J. *Give Me Liberty: The Christian Patriotism of Patrick Henry* (Leaders in Action). Cumberland House Publishing, 2002.

Walker, Gary C. *Civil War Tales: Volume II*. A & W Enterprise, 1994.

Washington, Booker T. *Up from Slavery*. New York: Dover Publications, 1995.

Waters-Power, Alma. *Virginia Giant: The Story of Peter Francisco*. New York: E.P. Dutton, 1957.

Wellman, Sam. *George Washington Carver: Inventor and Naturalist*. Barbour Publishing, 1998.

Wetterer, Margaret K. *Kate Shelley and the Midnight Express*. Scholastic, 1990.

Williams, Roger. *A Plea for Religious Liberty* in: *The Bloudy Tenant of Persecution*. Providence, Rhode Island: Narragansett Club, Vol. III, 1867.

Wrangel, Peter N. *Always with Honor*. New York: Robert Speller and Sons, 1957.

Websites

"Bill Overstreet." http://www.cebudanderson.com/billoverstreet.htm

"Bill Overstreet, 363rd FS." http://www.cebudanderson.com/overstreet.Htm

"Bill Overstreet: Barnstormers." http://www.barnstormers.com/eFLYER/2009/061-eFLYER-FA02-Legends-Overstreet.html

Winstead, Jane. "Horatio G. Spafford: The Story Behind the Hymn 'It is Well with My Soul.' " http://voices.yahoo.com/horatio-g-spafford-story-behind-hymn-is-1620793.html?cat=38.

Image Credits

Boldness

Col. John Mosby: Public Domain. Library of Congress: digital ID cwpbh.03240

Gen. Edwin Stoughton: Public Domain. U.S. Military images Photo courtesy of Mass Commander of MOLLUS

Gentleness

President Abraham Lincoln: Public Domain. Library of Congress, http://lcweb2.loc.gov/master/pnp/ppmsca/19300/19305u.tif

Old Naval Hospital: http://www.architectural-metal.com/the-old-naval-hospital-in-washington/

Initiative

Col. John Hunt Morgan: Public Domain. http://en.wikipedia.org/wiki/File:Gen._John_Morgan_%28cropped%29.jpg

Gen. Edward McCook: Public Domain. http://en.wikipedia.org/wiki/File:Edward_M._McCook_-_Brady-Handy.jpg

Morgan's Men: Public Domain. Hunt-Morgan House Deposit photographs, 1860-1949, housed at the University of Kentucky Special Collections and Digital Programs.

telegraph: Public Domain. http://www.history.army.mil/books/30-17/S_1.htm

Orderliness

Charles Marshall: Surrender at Appomattox Court House: http://www.historyofwar.org/Pictures/pictures_appomattox.html

Surrender document: Public Domain. National Archives and Records Administration, http://www.wildwestweb.net/cwdocs/surrender.html

Respectfulness

Francis Scott Key: Public Domain

Fort McHenry: http://members.tripod.com/~vet6_2/nationalanthem/natlanthem.html

Key on ship: http://the-english-spot.blogspot.com/2009_09_01_archive.html

Sensitivity

Robert E. Lee: Public Domain. http://en.wikipedia.org/wiki/File:General_R._E._Lee_and_Traveler.jpg

Tolerance

William Booth: Public Domain. http://salvos.org.au/hurstville/our-history/where-we-began/

"Salvation Army": Public Domain. http://baptistlandmarks.org/page93.html

Match factory: Public Domain. http://www.spartacus.schoolnet.co.uk/TUmatch2.jpg

Truthfulness

Sacagawea: Public Domain. http://www.sacagaweafacts.net/

Lewis and Clark: Public Domain. http://www.ohs.org/education/focus/lewis_and_clark_oregon.cfm

Virtue

Queen Victoria: Public Domain. presenting Bible: http://all-history.org/New%20Folder/341/10.jpg 'The Secret of England's Greatness' by Thomas Jones Barker

Queen Victoria with eldest daughter: Public Domain. http://en.wikipedia.org/wiki/File:Queen_Victoria_the_Princess_Royal_Victoria_c1844-5.png

Wisdom

Matthew Fontaine Maury: Public Domain. http://en.wikipedia.org/wiki/File:Matthew_Fontaine_Maury2.

About the Authors

Marilyn Boyer is the mother of fourteen children, all home schooled from kindergarten through high school. Her passion to train up her children in the character of Christ led her to create Character Concepts Curriculum, a character curriculum for kids of all ages to equip parents in raising children of integrity!

Her many character resources, as well as books on homeschooling and Christian parenting, are available online.

About the Authors

Grace Tumas Ehrman holds a degree in history from Liberty University. Her paper, "Warlords and Samurais: Japanese Interventionists in Siberia During the Russian Civil War, 1918-1922," won an award at the 2013 Phi Alpha Theta History Conference. She specializes in American and Russian history.